Idylls of the King and a Selection of Poems

"Though much is taken, much abides; and though
We are not now that strength which in old days
Moved earth and heaven, that which we are, we are;
One equal temper of heroic hearts,
Made weak by time and fate, but strong in will
To strive, to seek, to find, and not to yield."

Alfred Lord Tennyson

Anthony J. M. Brady - 2016

Anthony J. M. Brady

Homage to a Teacher

Selected Poems II

Cover: Petra Schubert

Editing: Petra Schubert

Photography: Petra Schubert

Publisher: tredition, Hamburg, Germany

ISBN

978-3-7469-4451-7 (Paperback)

978-3-7469-4452-4 (Hardcover)

978-3-7469-4453-1 (e-Book)

Contents

Contents

About the Author

Anthony J. M. Brady was born in 1940 in London. He retired in 1994, having completed a career in local government as a Principal Officer Team Leader with the London Borough of Camden, from whose Chief Executive's Department he had been seconded to the Department of Health & Social Security (Resettlement Centres) for 15 years. In 1997, he moved to Northern Ireland and lives in Brockagh, Tempo, Co. Fermanagh.

A Communitarian, he participates in part-time voluntary work involving social reconstruction, advocacy, renewal and reconciliation. His first writing in print was an essay in the London Chest Hospital Staff Magazine: Shakespeare and Medicine (1964). His first letter to a newspaper appeared in the Catholic Herald and this led to a series of polemical exchanges in its letter's page about the American/Vietnam War with the writer John Braine (1969/70). His first writing fee was for a book review: Caring on Skid Row by Anton Wallich-Clifford – the founder of The Simon Community, commissioned by The Catholic Herald (1974).

Subsequently, (1981-1986) he had letters published in The Catholic Universe, Hackney Gazette, The Guardian, The East Ender, The East London Mercury and The Greenwich Mercury on topics such as Apartheid; Drug Addiction; Homelessness and social justice issues. Many of his letters on topical issues have appeared in The Fermanagh Herald and The Impartial Reporter.

The Guardian printed four of his letters (1987-1990). One highlighted the threatened closure of a service for adolescent mentally ill people at The Maudsley Hospital; another two were arguments against reduction of hospital provision in London and the fourth objected to the euthanizing of the first person in England to have feeding methods legally withdrawn to assist his death.

A Paper entitled helping the Resettled Person with a Relapsing Drinking Problem was published by the Charity, Good Practices in Mental Health. ISBN 0 948445297

Tony began to send out creative work for the first time in 2003. A short story: 'Sister of Mercy' was published by the weekly magazine "Ireland's Own" and in 2004 an historical profile about Angela Burdett-Coutts: Queen of the Poor, was published by the bi-monthly magazine "Ireland's Eye". Both publications are popular in Ireland and the United States. Since 2003, he has had published (in anthology) numerous poems in various publications under the aegis of Forward Press: Anchor Books, Triumph House and New Poetry

Dogma Publications have also published his poetry in anthology. Other works comprise Castle Coole - Millennium Evocations - A National Trust house tour in verse.

In 2017, Tony's quartet of memoirs "Scenes from an Examined Life" has been published by tredition.co.uk.

In 2018, his "Homage to a Teacher, Selected Poems I", has been published by tredition.de.

Acknowledgements

I thank *Joan Major*, Head of European Languages Department, Fermanagh College, for her dedicated work in advancing Further Education. She made her French language academic expertise available to me in the completion of Castle Coole - Millenium Evocations, so preventing many literary *faux pas* on my account. *Muse*

Many thanks are due also to Joan's former College Lecturer colleague, inspirational *Nuala Corrigan*, who taught me Spanish and Italian, thereby stimulating my growing interest. *Mentor*

Michael O'Brien, whose publication of a selection of his poems - Intimations - in 2005, determined me to complete my "Homage to a Teacher". *Master*

Finally, none of the books in this series would have been produced without the dedication of *Petra Schubert* as my editor. *Motivator*

Introduction

When I was 15 years old, I left Salesian School, Blaisdon Hall, with no educational qualifications and went to work as a pig stockman on its Stud Farm, Blaisdon (Gloucestershire). My knowledge of poetry was having learned by repetition, poems that appealed mainly to my teachers. The earliest poem I committed to memory was *Daffodils* by *William Wordsworth*. From a very early age, I developed a facility for memorising poetry quickly - largely through fear, generated by a teacher in the first school I attended: St. George's, Gordon Road, Enfield. He taught English/Poetry, assisted by the medium of corporal punishment.

On the farm, while helping in the tractor maintenance shed, I vied with his knowledge of and traded poetry with *Brother Joseph Carter*. He declaimed passages from *Shakespeare's* plays; The Rime of the Ancient Mariner; Kubla Khan - Samuel Taylor Coleridge. The Deserted Village, - Oliver Goldsmith. Elegy - written in a country churchyard, - Thomas Gray. My riposte poetry was The Brook, The Lady of Shalott, - *Alfred Lord Tennyson. Abou Ben Adhem* (may his tribe increase) - *Leigh Hunt*, together with nonsense or bowdlerised verse from other classics that we made up. It all helped to pass the time and inject it with humour.

Lawrence Stanton, a fellow farm worker and chum loved poetry, read widely and fostered my interest in poetry and literature. As we hoed fodder beet, stacked hay and straw, riddled potatoes, dug ditches and trimmed hedges or lounged in each other's rooms, we would declaim all manner of poems to each other and could quote extensively. In the same way of matching quote for quote with *Bro. Joe,* so it was in a similar but not competitive manner between Lawrence and me. It was only when I decided to make good the deficit in my formal educational qualifications through attending night classes, in the East End of London, where I lived from aged 23, that a guided critical appreciation for poetry was stimulated. I had attempted to write poems to please myself while on the farm, but never actually showed them to anyone.

With formal teaching of English literature, I was exposed to an intense critical analysis of the written text with the purpose of understanding the *structure* of the poetry, with less attention given to the meaning and purposes of the author. I learned that a description of scenes from nature or the expression of emotions was multi-layered, and was best communicated by a particular set of rules which, constituted *form.* So devices, such as iambic pentameter, scansion, enjambment, sonnet form, rhyming couplets, and effects such as alliteration, onomatopoeia, metaphor and metre and the ability to recognise these in the poetry's structure was what examiners sought.

I worked and studied hard in the night school and luckily for me, I had a teacher who was very encouraging: *Miss. Mary Wilkinson.* Not long graduated from Oxford University and inspired with a mission to work in the educationally deprived East End of London, she came to a day further education college and got me to join her English Language and English Literature classes there also.

Mary Wilkinson was younger than me and I was soon much smitten by her. However, I remained the intensely shy person I was in Blaisdon when it came to interacting with the female sex but managed to express subtle unrequited longings about her in my essays and literary criticism of the poems she set. However, I did drop my guard once when she invited her class students to extemporise a poem, on a theme of love, in 20 minutes against the clock. I learned from Miss. Wilkinson that the most perfect line of English poetry is *Edmund Spenser's*: "Flow gently sweet Thames until I end my song." This is because it observes all the rules of form, metre etc., alluded to earlier. She also told me that the most perfect introductory line of prose - in relation to its setting - is found in the opening lines of *Daphne du Maurier's* novel Rebecca: "Last night I dreamt that I went to Manderley again". Miss. Wilkinson said she was not expressing a personal opinion here but only passing on to her students the received wisdom of the most perceptive critics. She asked what I considered a close comparison - having regard to the determining criteria - of this perfectly expressed poetry and prose. I chose a passage from Hamlet: "*There is a Divinity that shapes our ends - rough hew them how we will.*"

This Collection is dedicated to my children Laura, Paul, Christian and all teachers.

Castle Coole

First Sight

Along a grand drive
In an avenue of oaks
Near a still Lough
Stands Castle Coole
Neo-classical - Wyatt's jewel

Embossed is a rose
On columns Ionic
Keeping sentinel stately
With fluted pillars - Doric
Every stone sublimely historic

Lion-headed doors open
Into the Grand Hall
Lyceum, temple, shrine
All Greek and Roman in style
You enter: Art and Artifice beguile

Castle Coole Dedication

For You, as you recall your visit's pleasure
In keep-sake form to later read and treasure
I, led by Beauty, these few verses framed
On Castle Coole, this house most famed
Of absent architect James Wyatt, who's fine
Neo-classical ideals here witness his design
Lauded in all Ireland for its style and grace
I revere likewise those, whose emblems grace
Chalice, wreath, the rose, in Portland stone
On plaster, wood, metal and patterned bone
China, the eminence of a noble line, evermore:
Armar/Lowry/Corry to present Earl Belmore

In this Millennium may time to You and His be kind
And all who visit here renewed love of Beauty find

The Morning Room

As the sun came up, the family came down
To breakfast: scones, scrambled egg, bacon
Left warm upon the rosewood sideboard
While the butler from the nearby pantry
Brought coffee, milk and tea

Now used as the present Earl's art gallery
A selection only… Here visitors can peer
At his finest oil paintings while waiting
Under Joseph Rose's ornate corniced ceiling
For their marvelling house tour to begin

In a pagoda-style cabinet hung with bells
Half a set of Chelsea ware is on view
The rest, a helpful guide tells, was gifted
As a dowry later, in lieu of taxes
Sadly sold from Florence Court

A painting by Cipriani (1783) dominates
One wall: the Greek myth depicted shows
Castor and Pollux: destined to be stars
They pose in human form - armed and disarmed

Over the marble fireplace, the oldest picture
Displayed shows a biblical theme:
The Rest on the Flight to Egypt; for years
Mary was a single mother until its cleaning
Revealed Joseph, her smoke obscured spouse

The Second Earl, who furnished Castle Coole
Is portrayed by Douglas Hamilton in full pose, erect
One hand bears a Petition on The Act of Union
Which he opposed: holding out against it by honour
Bound to ancestral exclusion from The House of Lords

Here in this house, family Honour, Duty, Style
And Beauty rest enshrined: from the windows
The cricket pitch confirms the state of play
The noble Belmore family observes

In the open Visitor's Book is written:
"Timeless Beauty -unequalled!"

The Entrance Hall

Pause: gaze high before
East entry: a notable absence
The style has it secrets
The mechanical camouflaged
All gutters and down-pipes
By limestone buttress concealed

Corry, Lowry, Belmore
Ancestral in marble, on stucco
Their emblems are chased: rose
Wreath and chalice in frieze
And on fireplace, gadrooned
Torchieres, harmonious space

Two tall windows, two niches
A Portland stone floor:
Mahogany chairs splay-footed
Four equidistant: true doors
Pivot on weights hidden in walls
Trompe-l 'oeil others directly opposed

Art and artifice - the true or
The feigned and Westmacott's
Carving cut from Carrara
Bartoli's Ionic pillars - mock marble
Scagliola secretly wrought
Stand single and opposed

Innate truths - gratuitous ornament
The angles of vision inspire
Symmetrical, you see depth in Beauty
Uniting Reason, ordered values
Classical themes defining forms
Logically transfigured in Time

The Library

You pass through double doors and secret device
Into Regency style, the Second Earl's taste
By John Preston rendered; Two of everything?
Portraits by Pooley, Jervas: a pair by Gascars
Louise de Kérouaille, French beauty *en balcon:*
Duchess of Portsmouth, her title by King Charles
The Second bestowed: "*For services rendered*"
Her detractors opined; alongside, a boy
Of six years imperially toga clad
Her son by "*The King Over The Water*"
Later Duke of Richmond: plays, poetry, painting
And horse-racing in his patronage flourished

Red silken curtains cascade from golden pelmet:
Centrally a wreath divides griffon's head finials
Above one of two Egyptian-style-couches a burial
Urn by a carved black elephant bearing an obelisk
High on a bookcase broods a bust by Turelli:
Duke of Wellington, Iron Duke, irony in marble
Victor, though Dublin born, "*The Greatest Englishman!*"
Shouted the London mob: Wreath browed, proudly
It peers at tributes and metaphors of his Nile success

Eastern carpet, a pair of Corinthian columned lights
Twin globes: terrestrial and celestial right and left
Of marble fire surround whose chiselled drapery by
Westmacott echoes the sumptuous window drapes
Porcelain: Worcester and Derbyshire in pairs
Books by the yard encased all leather bound
A carved marble cherub on classical desk

A prancing bronze horse paperweight
Another statue from which all equine form
In Art derives: The Colleoni after Verrocchio
A horse in a 1950's Belmore family portrait
By Derek Hill: a young girl astride it outside
The windows of The Saloon, seated at his
Parent's feet - the now Eighth Earl

The Staircase Hall

Regency diversions by mahogany twin doors
To meet pure neo-Classical presence at height
Of its style: two polished pillars *engaged* on
Each wall from Portland stone floor rise marble
Based to stairs, high gallery: The Lobby

Over the main doors: a half moon window
Latticed light trap: its spider's web tracery
Recalls mythical Arachne; a single flight ascends
While buttressed beneath the Butler's Stair descends
Into Servant's rooms and tunnel to stables…

On either side, mahogany Belmore chairs by Kidd
That Wyatt designed: curved, crafted compliment
To turned wooden banisters; underhand, their twirls
Enclose an ebony circle marking in time and place
Joiner's joy at wages paid at the Spot and on the Dot

Each step flanked by roses in ironwork rises to stone
Half-landing, - then, double return stairs cantilevered
Melded in walls corniced with bull's skulls, alluded in
Bas relief plasters The Minotaur - labyrinth slain: bulls
From Poseidon's temple all recalled in detail from
James Wyatt's 1772 London Pantheon…

The Lobby

Through double mahogany doors
To formal reception: a square space
At your feet pale oaken floors
Triple glass domes make place
On high for natural light
Defining all by day and night

Exquisite mouldings in plaster
Ceiling: cast by Rose the master
In stucco, quite as Wyatt designed
A chalice, its handles entwined
By a rose, the classical wreath
All family symbols in bas-relief

Above, a railed gallery four square
Reached by a stone servant's stair
Leads to private rooms unseen
Of family domicile and between
The columned walk espy standing
A wooden telescope upon a landing

Four alcoved pedestal stoves in white
Faux-vrais stand opposed at chest height
The true fires peaty smoke congealed
In flues plastered corners concealed
Corniced ram's heads droop while chairs
Roped, stand in equidistant pairs

Moulded architraves aside each door
In perfect counterpoint to oaken floor
Leading left to The Bow Room and
Right to the King's State Bedroom
En face to the Servant's Staircase
And behind the Grand Staircase

The North West Bedroom & Dressing Room

Once the bedroom of Honaria
Wife of Somerset Richard, The Fourth Earl
A niece of a British Prime Minister
William Ewart Gladstone, she was the mother
Of thirteen children, two portraits of her
In youthful, then mature beauty grace
The hand block painted wallpaper

The room is a preserving repository
Of generations of children's toys
The sense of family and its humanity
Abounds and is visualised here more
Than in any other room in Castle Coole
Contrast a rocking-horse and teddy bear
With a toy emu and kangaroo recalling family
Sojourn in Australia on Empire duties

In a doll's house presented by the people
To Belmore family serving in Queensland
The Governor's domestic life is in miniature
Displayed to the extent of wallpaper used

In the State House lining its tiny walls
Once bulging leather luggage is retained:
Here a Gladstone bag, there a Louis Vuitton
Hat bag circa 1890, timeless ultimate accessory

A four-poster canopy bed is matched by another
In an en suite dressing room: saved from Queen Anne
House - the windows overlook its site long destroyed
Now the oldest piece of furniture in the house
It's carved from bog wood Grinling Gibbons could
Have influenced and would have coveted
Out from under its coverlet one imagines a Lord
Leaping into the adjacent hip bath by the open fire

Not so perhaps; surmising about the riding
Boots with crop to hand suggests a horse
Already saddled in the stable yard, - beware
Then, any creature fleet of foot and furry
As the morning chase got under way; through
Fields and drumlin, by hills and lough in
Swiftly lifting mists, the land was clear
To hunt: seventy thousand acres in its day

The State Bedroom

King George, The Fourth
While visiting the North
Of his Union Irish state
In 1821 was wont to indicate
A Castle Coole stay might beguile
His penchant for the latest style
So, the Second Earl spent
Lavishly with every intent
To impress; John Preston
Best internal decorator, did the rest
Engaging Dublin's finest, who made
Manifest all plans the Earl had laid

Alas! The King awaited, went
Off to County Meath and spent
Much time in courtesans embrace
At Slane Castle, so never came to grace
This room with regal repose or ease
At his disposal everything designed to impress

There, seductive silken splendour gold and red
With goldthread swags hang about the bed
Unused since that time of royal visit planned
While curtained windows eastward facing stand
Shuttered forever lest natural light fall
And sumptuous silken canopy's tassels pall
Feet of lions carved in Spanish mahogany paw
The carpet, bearing bed corners on polished claw

And over rosewood steps at pillow side ascending
Are tasselled bell pulls in woven silk descending
On red flock papered walls to plaster cornice trimmed
And ceiling all adorned - whitewashed limned
Marble-topped sideboards polished bright
Reflect Corinthian columned candle's light
That falls on Georgian table where is laid
A Crown Derby porcelain inkwell uniquely made
For royal use; likewise, a carved wood brass-bound
Box where ready trimmed writing quills are found

The Bow Room

Lady Belmore's bower of beauty
Boudoir of elegance where duty
Determined the latest of style:
Queen Anne, Georgian, Regency, while
Tapestry on round table recaptured
Times when a golden harp enraptured

The refining influence of women
Through music, paintings, ceramics
Enfolds all in silken chinoiserie
At draped bow windows, in wallpaper
In a bamboo suite of exquisite fragility
On gros-point carpet and rattan flooring

The view from the casement windows
Takes in an arc The Park's broad sweep:
Lough Coole, distant Cole Memorial
Belmore Mountain, The Drive flanked with oaks
Clusters of elm, sycamore, a walled Ha-Ha
All framed in capitals of Corinthian columns

Books in cases, each side of the fireplace:
Raided from the Library - a liberation of
Feminist forces by literature unleashed
Grace and decorum in delicate Chinese fans
To protect women's wax make up and faces from
Hearth's heat: beauty cooled by wave of a hand

Fourteen engravings, by Vernet of French ports
In readiness for war: the French Revolution (1789)
Occurred while Castle Coole was abuilding and
All Ireland trembled; four watercolours, on loan
By Cassas, his pupil, recall lost civilisations
Hone's: Pont du Gard, in oils holds the declension

Castle Coole women: in imagination, you walk
To the windows, on Queen Anne settees you talk
Your fingers embroid, round the piano you sing
Sweet music and pluck plangent on harp string
Themes echoing eternal from those distant days
Enchanting us still - by the grace of your ways

The Dining Room

Here, unvisited by him, see ordered harmony refined:
James Wyatt's vision all combined
In plaster, metal, marble, glass
Textile, wood, elements of solid mass
Balance lightest beauty in architecture
Hold classical allusion from literature
And reflect from gilded silver burnish
Engraved Belmore motto: *Virtus Semper Viridis*

Virtue Ever Untarnished: family silver unsold
Upon the sideboard proudly shines in gold
And pagan mythology etched in filigreed plate
Depicts *The Abduction of Europa*: from state
Of Arcadian innocence borne to Cretan shores
She hangs on garlanded neck of bull-feigned Zeus
Alongside, identical ornate Grecian urns rest
On polished pedestals - grisaille leather impressed
Beneath this mahogany sideboard so finely tooled
A carved sarcophagus - lead lined, where wine was cooled
Resides: monument to Barnie & Bernie, carvers, who wrought

Its shape from a single block of mahogany brought
It's said, from Hispaniola; Lough Coole ice refreshed
The summer glass of visitor and household guest
When brought from Ice House, built in the demesne
To sparkle, wink and bubble as a blushful Hippocrene

The dining table edge on brassbound pedestals gleaming
Reflects the curved chair-back head's carved reaming
And on two matching mahogany pier tables, in place
Each side of marble fireplace, fine dishes grace
Both surfaces matching the porcelain made
Of Crown Derby, green and white, already laid
As light thro' translucent green Bohemian glasses
From carved cupola headed casement windows passes

Lifespan dated portraits of ancestor's faces
Look down on what were once familiar places
At table or gaze on carved oak-leaf and acorn
Loved by the Second Earl's wife: they adorn
The doorposts, reminding her of cherished trees
That lined the drive to Castle Coole; "Please
Rise to toast the genius of James Wyatt!" The Queen
Mother, dining here proposed; Masterpiece he had never seen

The Drawing Room

Out of shadowed Inner Hall
Into female sanctum: *en face*
Voiled sash windows; light falls
On oaken floor and papered walls
In blue, taste à *la mode* recalls
Versailles's mirrored halls

French formality, elegant Empire style
Pink silk day beds designed to while
Temps passant as The Three Fates smile
Where drum clock's brass shows trial
Of Life's thread spun from Clotho's spool
Lachesis's measure, Atropos's snipped denial

Exquisite chandelier, where black fauns swing
Above Aubusson carpet; Dresden ewers bring
Images of Air and Water by mirrors echoing
*Á la belle époqu*e the gentlemen's approving
Glance on petticoated ankles revealed moving
In dancing or by Louis Quatorze medallion cabinet posing

Would that those people on the walls portrayed
Could by some magic incantation, their death gainsaid
Return and round the circular table, boule inlaid
Converse again or by the marble hearth parade
Anew, they would not *un moment* be uneasy or dismayed
Such is the preserved beauty here on view

Helas!
Tous viennent. Tous restent. Tous passent.
Mais ceux qui y visitent en émerveillent.

The Saloon

Oval
Shaped room
Cuban mahogany doors
With inlaid grisaille panels
By Biaggio Rebecca and carved
To match the curvature of walls and
Backs of silken settees; a Broadwood
Piano (1802) restored: its keyboard faced
With tiles of classical scenes in Wedgwood
Adjacent to it an Irish harp by a brass inlaid
Circular table, Boule, one of a pair; two black
Ornate iron working stoves topped by Grecian
The urns are fixed to secret flues; gilded original
Mirrors and torchieres by Wyatt, Crown glass
In windows reach to ornate white ceiling, this
Italianate Saloon is said to be inspired by a
Barbarini house in Rome; Florence trained
Bartoli crafted marbled black and white
Pilasters; Great ceiling high windows
Soar to Rose's defining shape and
Lead directly onto lawns, where
Dancers swayed into moonlight
Reflecting off Lough Coole
Till dawn light filtered
Through the branches
Of the distant
Trees

Envoi

Great doors close, the group divides:
Down smooth worn steps each tread
Leads over gravel sound that guides
Your path to Stable Yard; see spread
Before you ancient fields, all green
Where drumlin forms a natural scene
About Lough Coole set in park demesne

Glance briefly back to look again
On fluted Doric columned colonnade
At entry where lion heads maintain
Sentry under roofline balustrade
Marvel at the symmetry whose style
Harmony, balance and scale beguile
You, then slowly turn away and smile

Farewell, though distance decrease
Sight of present Beauty its joy will
Last forever; its loveliness increase
As memories return to stir and fill
Again your sight and senses; to fuel
Anew love of Classic forms that rule
In purest sway at noble Castle Coole

Genesis of Castle Coole Poems

Over three years until 2000, I was a seasonal House Guide in the National Trust property Castle Coole. Situated close to the city of Enniskillen, County Fermanagh, it is the ancestral home of the noble Earls of the Belmore family. On rest days, the manager at the time organised educational mini-bus trips to other National Trust properties in Northern Ireland. On the long journeys, poetry was recited among the guides as a form of amusement. The manager - more joking than serious - suggested that I write the Castle Coole House tour in verse. A visitor had written in the Visitor's Book: *"Mr. Brady's tour is pure poetry..."*

To mark the significance of the year 2000 was important. It took some time to compose the poems, which eventually formed a booklet entitled: *"Castle Coole – Millennium Evocations"*. It was intended to be a "time capsule", in which each of the rooms open to the public is described with accurate reference to the art and artefacts in position at the time. The name of the mentoring manager is in acrostic form in the poem – First Sight.

Much help was received from The National Trust, and I was allowed to accompany each poem with a portrait of each of the rooms described. Later, I presented the 7th Earl John Belmore with the completed work, which included a refreshed historical profile of James Wyatt. It has been archived in the Enniskillen Library for inclusion in the preserved history of Castle Coole.

In 2012, again aided by The National Trust, the book was professionally printed in a limited edition. It was promoted as a fund raiser for a local charity - Children of Chernobyl - which brings children affected by accidental nuclear radiation from Belarus, Ukraine, for holiday breaks with families in County Fermanagh. Copies may still be available from The Stables - *Once Loved Books* - Shop in Castle Coole.

Humour

It is easy to claim that humorous poems are a crime against poetry. We are all familiar with poems that tell jokes, poems that are extended puns or just fail to impress as limp limericks. Criticising these poems is easy. What I attempt is satire and irony poems: satire and irony make people laugh. But the undertone to such poems is always serious. To be dismissive of them is to be blind to the possibility of serious art that is funny.

I particularly like parody. It allows me take an already existing prose piece or poem as a scaffold, and making it humorous by changing the language, while keeping within the style of the original way it is written. It is a technique I practice, and it has definitely helped expand my poetry writing skills. The examples I included are mostly topical/political parody. They are survivors of ephemera that I have sprayed onto the internet, under the pen-name Tobias or as blogs: mainly in *The Guardian* and *The Independent* newspapers.

Laughing at funny poems helps us get through the bad times and get to the good. Whatever the words or sayings, we can sit back and smile or have a good laugh and not have our worries bother us.

Hilarious poems are lovable. They make us smile, while passing along a message, which is unforgettable. Not to mention that everyone loves to read something that makes us laugh every now and then. It releases stress and gives us something to smile about after a rough day at work or school.

Gotta Get Me Some Protection

Oh, Dear! What can the matter be?
Johnny Scarlotti is following me…
He won't buy a trinket to please me
But with a smile would ease me
Onto a slab at the morgue

Oh, Dear! What can the matter be?
Johnny's on his way from the fair
He's bringing me a basket of posies
A garland of lilies, a bunch of red roses
A wreath for where my body reposes

Oh, Dear! What can the matter be?
Johnny Scarlotti* is following me...

**A cult poet – symbolic chain-saw wielding*

After Snowden

A password forgetter I knew
Asked me what could they do?
I thought for a while
Then said with a wry smile
"Just get on the phone to GCHQ!"

While reviewing new battle ships
In fleet form on the river Rhine
Angela Merkel, wanting to dine
Ordered on her mobile calamari
Then overheard Barack Obama
Suggest doughnuts, pizza and dips

Angela retorted with "Aw! Gee!
Barack, I know what you had for tea
According to my twitters
At breakfast Putin had fritters
You're wearing red boxers - I'm told;
Michelle's choice of knickers is gold."

Flop Gear

Has a petrol-head – call him Claxton
Run out of speedy road to park on?
Because of his late meal
His producer got a weal
Now his fans wail: *"Oh Dear!*
It's a dead end for "TOP GEAR"

Seems the wheels have come off
For this brazen non-PC toff
Is it the end of the ride
For Chipping Norton's pride
And no clear Right of Way

No sensible man would scupper
His own TV slot for a cold supper
Yet there's alpha males who dread
TOP GEAR'S due for a feminist re-tread
Go girls! Vroom! Vroom! Time for you instead

Asking For It

A fit-looking tramp
Just out of prison
Called at a house
And asked for help
"I'm surprised at
A man like you
asking for money!"
Said the lady
Of the house

"I've got to ask
For it ma'am."
He replied
"When I took
It last time
Without asking
I got six
Months inside."

Head And Shoulders

The last time
I was in Italy
I went into a
Florence Barber's
Shop for a shampoo
The assistant enquired
Where I came from
I told him - "*Ireland*"
When he asked me
For my name
I said "*Tim O'Tay*"

"Prego Signore.
Tell me yours!"
I asked
He replied -
"*Alberto Balsam!*"

Head For Bread

Mine host in a B&B on the coast
Excelled in the making of toast
But one morning - half awake
He made this mistake:
Instead of bread
He toasted his head
I assure you, no take-on
His patrons thought it was bacon

Not Wot Wordsworth Wrote

Daffodils?
Wordsworth's waved and danced:
Mine just bend, bow and nod
In a sight, densely displayed
Upon a mossy bank

No lake there, nor cloud
In the sky, neither am I lonely
I'm here with a girl called April
Counting those yellow heads
Is easy: sixty, if I'm not mistaken

How William *"...saw ten thousand*
At a glance.." from a closet, baffles me
It seems daffodils make you gay
And sprightly dance - jocund too
At least they made him so

Now supine upon my comfy couch
I lie - in breezy mood of parody
It transports me off to Holland
Where in Amsterdam counting tulips
Naughty Weekend April is beside me

Nothing Personal

Royal baby Charlotte! Why the fuss?
What's she ever done for us?
Half the nation's overweight. Zounds!
She's already piling on the pounds

Alas! Great-Grand-Queen-Mother Lizzie
Is not around to order up the fizzy
Hushabye! Like RIP Backstairs Billy, true
Nanny will be always there for you

Food banks you will never know
Nor will you shop in Lidl or Tesco
Still, there will always be a queue
Of eager suitors lining up for you

So sleep pretty babe - don't frown
In future you might wear a crown
But, just for now, a wee white bonnet:
HER ROYAL HIGHNESS knitted neatly on it

Porridge Ode

I will arise and forage
Not for eggs nor bread
For a bowl of porridge
That gets me out of bed

Smooth like silk
With added milk
Not lumpy mind
'Tis good to find
It thick and grey
No better way
To start the day

If the spoon stands upright
No need to get uptight
It passed the test
Of thin or thick
Got the Tick
The Best

Top Recipe:
Take Slade Prison
Add Ronnie Barker
& Richard Beckinsale
Stir in Fulton Mackay
Mr. Barrowclough to serve

Saint Patrick

Saint Patrick, to Fermanagh came once more:
Off Devenish Island, he swam ashore
Waiting there was an eager crowd
Priest and Laity roaring loud

St. Patrick smiled, then kneeling there
Bowed his tousled head in prayer
"God Bless you one and all," he said:
"Grace and Mercy on the quick and dead."

St. Patrick, cold from Lough Erne surf
Warmed himself by a glowing fire of turf
Father D'Arcy gave out shamrock tea
Soda bread, buttered scones and homily

"Any questions?" the fêted Saint enquired
"Yes!" said someone, just then inspired
"Has Ian Paisley been rejected
Or, now among Heaven's elected?"

St. Patrick answered "No problem whatever
But until he stops shouting 'Never! Never!'
At St. Peter's call, to enter ere the gates
In Purgatory, pastor Ian impatiently waits

Next year, I will be back and fill
You in on his celestial fate, so I will
You know, I never really went away
Great to greet you on this special day."

With that, St. Patrick ascended on a cloud
While the awestruck watching crowd
To praise, revere and honour him
Sang out the rare traditional hymn
"Hail! Glorious Saint Patrick"

A Spanish Song

Close by the Mission San Cristòbal
Is a great house wherein dwells
The distant, cool and beguiling
La Doña Carmen Garcia-Cabrall

At her command I saddle the mare
I ride behind and attend as she
Visits her friends here and there
La Doña Carmen Garcia-Cabrall

She say: "Harness my horse - Miguel!
Bring my boots - Miguel!
Thank you - Miguel." I obey all for
La Doña Carmen Garcia-Cabrall

Her lover Don José Francisco Delgado
Is often away: He say: "Adios!
Miguel! And be sure to watch over
La Doña Carmen Garcia-Cabrall!"

Close by the Mission San Cristòbal
I wait in the yard of the great
House wherein dwells
La Doña Carmen Garcia-Cabrall

She say: "Stable the horse - Miguel!
Then come upstairs: Quickly! - Miguel!
Now pull my boots off - Miguel!
Thank you - Miguel!"

I say: "Señora! Is that all?"
She say: "Do as you wish Miguel! –
Miguel - Bolt the door!"
La Doña Carmen Garcia-Cabrall

The Pearly Gates

When I arrive at The Pearly Gates
I will still be troubled by
The one thing in life I never
Really understood: I mean
The second Theory of Relativity
My nightmare is that St. Peter
Is not on duty the day I die
And I seek entry
He will have, I hope, passed
On the usual questions
All of which I have sure-fire
Prepared answers to one
Of his locum guardians
Hope it's not Albert Einstein

The Singing Chef

I entered school at Blaisdon Hall
When everybody seemed so tall:
But when I finished being taught
All my chums in height were short

The invention of a former cook
Fed the progress of my build and look
Along with spuds - best of Stud Farm crop
And regular pudding known as "FLOP"

Wilfred Higginbotham was his name:
T'was from Manchester that he came
Before him the chef was Mr. Higgins:
Toupee-topped, nicknamed “Wiggins”

Very wobbly on a pushbike:
Wilfred was (as they say today) "like"
Sort of fat, yet, tha' knows
Very light upon his toes

If in the mood and no kerfuffle
He'd do a lively soft shoe shuffle
Opera trained - Wilfred was a singer:
For a famous Welsh tenor a dead ringer

By the serving hatch, his apron gravy stained
Melodious, cheerful, unrestrained
He'd make the pots and kettles ring
As from the repertoire he'd gaily sing

Selections de La Traviata, La Boheme
In his opinion "la crème de la crème"
And other classic arias with aplomb
In the style of Harry Secombe

Now Wilfred's "FLOP": a sort of Madeira cake
From the kitchen hatch the server would take
A warmish, deep presenting tray
Where puffed up inviting, there it lay

Father "Bulldog" Wilson then would cut a slice
Take a bite - declare it "Nice!"
Alas! His knife released the air
That wily Wilf had mixed in there

Like a balloon pricked by a pin
Silently within the cooling tin
The cake collapsed, what a Hump!
Wilf (t'was said) had used a stirrup pump

Wilfred - as a baker- didn't cut the mustard
But he was a dab hand when it came to custard
A portion of his added magic yellow liquor
Made the deflated "Flop!" taste thicker

What was served up, had a fleeting taste
And was scoffed down in a fitful haste
Thus pleased, I am here to relate
Not a trace of "FLOP!" was left upon the plate

Whatever came of Wilf, I'll never know:
Back up North, to ailing mum he had to go
But still his pudding can invoke
Such sensual sentiments all beyond a joke

Early on in life Marcel Proust's nibbled madelaine
A lifetime later, when dipped in tea
And tasted once again, had power to regain
Lost time and illuminate his memory

So it is with me and as I thought
Of cher Marcel, an evocative poem was wrought:
"FLOP"!" inspires the 1950s when I recall
Those schoolboy meals in Blaisdon Hall

Tryst With A Twist

A limo parks up in a silent street:
Moonlight filters into a hotel suite
Naked a form lies under a flimsy sheet
A door opens and quickly closes
Furtively to the bed a figure moseys
Slipping in beside the dozer
Snuggled up, ever closer
He whispers "Julia, I need you;
You waited. I love you."
Suddenly the tryst is broken
As deep voiced words are spoken:
"Who is Julia?"
"I'm Julian..."

The Useless Boob

And God created Woman
And she was good
And she had two arms
Two legs and three breasts

God asked Woman
What she would like
To have changed about herself?
And she asked for her
Middle breast to be removed

God removed her middle breast
And it was good…

She stood there with
Her third breast in her
Hand and asked God
What should be done
With this useless boob?

Then God created Man…

Life

Thanks to a long life, I am the sum of all the experiences that I have encountered. Day to day struggles and triumphs are experienced by all creatures that occupy this world of existence. Not for nothing is Life poetically described as a journey. Through poetry, I have shared experiences common to all thinkers on the journey of Life.

As human beings, when we encounter a challenge, we face it with the limited freedom of choice that determines how we react. Every decision that we make leads us down a different road. Whatever the signposts and landmarks, we never arrive at our destination with identical experiences of those on the same road.

"We shall not cease from exploration, and the end of all our exploring will be to arrive where we started and know the place for the first time." *

Poetry has the power to convey the forces that, like great winds, blow us hither and thither, until we reach our destination. Poetry has given me certainties in life: it has acted as a compass. Poetry is an exploration of the spirit. From eager youth to the now threshold of octogenarian quietude, I have not ceased from exploring.

"Old men ought to be explorers. Here or there does not matter. We must be still and still moving - into another intensity. For a further union, a deeper communion. Through the dark cold and the empty desolation: the wave cry, the wind cry, the vast waters of the petrel and the porpoise. In my end is my beginning." **

T. S. Eliot, The Four Quartets: * *Little Gidding* ** *East Coker*

A Ticking Clock

Homeless: after midnight
Sheltered in this cold
Church doorway
I can hear a clock
Ticking in its tower

Rustling leaves, tossed
Along wet pavement
In a callous wind sound
Like approaching footsteps

In famished sleep
I dream of former glory
Me: A celebrity
Yeah! – Big Time…

All I have now
Are fading echoes
Of cheering crowds
Some comfort

The applause dies
I awake: alone with
Sounds: a clock ticking
Leaf blown footsteps
A cheerless wind

Forgive And Forget

To

Truly

Forgive

Someone

Who harmed

You, is to Forget

Where you buried

The avenging hatchet

Hospital Poem

Now is a good time to be ill:
A room with a view
Over Wolf Lough awaits
Here human life starts
Is prolonged and ends

The old Erne dies:
A new hospital comes to life
No wards - single rooms
For patients - while they stay
For nursing back to health

Here are long serving doctor's dreams
Realised in glass and steel:
Every form of clinical hi-tech
Is in situ; recovery comfort aids
In reach of nurse and patient

Awesomely experienced doctors attend:
"A pain in the belly?" Call Dr. Kelly
"Disrupted cardiac karma?" Call Dr. Varma
"Car crash shaken chakras?" Call Dr. Rahman
Coming up for air? Call Dr. McClaire
Now is a good time to be ill

The Queen, in June 2012
Snipped a ribbon in ceremony:
"I declare the SWAH - 'You What?'
Is now open! Goodness Gracious Me!
Just call it The Jubilee."

Orison

God
Of Man
Woman, Soul
Thank you for creating me

You
Called me from sleep
To meet this day
Whatever comes or may

To
You I offer all
My actions: let them
Be done as Thou will

For
Thy greater glory
Keep me from sin
And every evil

May
Thy Grace be always
With me and all those
Dear to me

Amen

Fears

It used to frighten me at night
A young farmer then
The bull would break out

I would take my blanket
And in practice play
The matador's moves

It was my way
Of countering my fears
Of a horned charge in the night

It never came
But being ever ready
I slept always on guard

Monday

Monday: an orange sky
Rays refreshing wilting flowers
Singed by a candle flame
In a blue china bowl

Prisoner

Upon that little tent of blue
We prisoners call the sky
My tormented thoughts of you
Smother words, provoke a sigh

My iron bed provides no rest
I made it for myself. Alas!
Maybe it's for the best
Served time must pass

My sins none can forgive
A penitent I remain
In solitary I live
A man who all distain

Roadkill

Near a green hollow where a ditch runs
It lies off road: grassy fronds toss
Shade back towards the sun's
Rays that fall on cushioning moss

Hit by a passing vehicle - I surmise…

A badger, mouth open, jet hair
Bathed in blue water cress
Seems asleep, white blazed, unaware
Of clouds and wind's caress

On closer look - a grim surprise…

Like a stroller taking a rest
Its nostrils uncloyed by scents
Motionless, laid out on its chest
In its right side are two red rents

Lead-shot peppers an entry wound…

Seeds Strewn On Eager soil

Seeds strewn on eager soil
Seem to die into dust
Dissipate into air
Over the meadows

Seeds burst open
Creeping green stems
Stretch advancing out
Covering the ground

Time passes:
Stems form stalks
They sway in the breeze
Rainfall and sunshine

Spring arrives:
Countless colours
Emerge as green carpet
Covering the meadows

Buds burst into flower
Grounded in roots
Fragile yet firm holding
They dance in the wind

Meadow mown hay
In verdant swathes
Lie in snaking wispy lines
New seeds will germinate
Harboured until Spring

Teatime

"Lance Corporal -
Your turn to brew up."
"Aye. So it is Sergeant."
Lightning shrieks…
Thunder of guns…

Angels weep before
Enraged Gods
Spilt tea upon the ground:
Crushed urn upended
Poet Ledwidge lying dead
Bomb-blasted

The sky is grey –
Earth bloody red
White crosses clutched
Tighter than triggers

The cause unknown…
Excuses made…
Lives of the wounded
Set for a slow declining

The irony is – we live
That's what we are dying for

The Hour

Where does it go:
That hour
When clocks
Go back
Or forward?

Does time stop
To welcome
Winter in
Bidding the
Summer - farewell?

No: sleep lost
Or gained
Holds secret
The time
And the hour

Change as you
May hands of
Watch or clock:
The sundial shadow
Falls unaltered

"The Cruellest Month" - Not For Me

Pastoral peace pervades fields and dells:

On boughs, in hedges, birds rehearse

Their euphoric trills - each note tells

Of will to mate in tones desiring, terse

Sun rays filter through April showers

Tinting daffodils with yellow gold

Coaxing to bloom perennial flowers

Easter lambs bleat from sheltered fold

Eager to stray and play by rising streams

Winding over meadows to mill ponds

Where moorhens nest and idle angler dreams

Rabbits appear from cover of ferny fronds

While in the trees countless leafy voices

Sigh soothingly as all of Nature rejoices

A Mother's Love

Your love is like an
Atoll in life's ocean
Vast and wide:
A haven, calm shelter
From the wind, the rain, the tide
It's bound on the north by Hope
By Patience on the West
By tender Counsel on the South
And on the East by Rest
Over it a beacon flame
Reflects Faith, Truth, Prayer
While from all the raging
Storms of life - your children
Find a sanctuary there

Without You

I have tried to imagine my world without you:
Summer swarming bees, distant Cotswold peaks
Hidden in snow; the beauty of autumn mornings
Along Blaisdon's remembered country roads
A sunlit river Severn beyond Westbury, the
Whirr of pheasants at spring midday and
The calling of owls towards midnight

Now I know that none of it is the same
Without you, but most of all I will never
Forget your smile, your eyes, your
Gentleness and giving, your loyalty
And caring for old friends: Len Carter
Frank and Elsie Hogg, in particular
The memories we treasured, the
Enjoyments we shared…

The love is forever there, despite time or distance
Clarified through tears, so today I celebrate that
You existed; thanking all of life for your life
Expressing my deepest gratitude that out of
Millions of people and possibilities
Our lives were destined to be intermingled

As in sorrow, I mourn your passing
I know clearly and forever my world
Can never be the same: Without You

Zeitfracht Medien GmbH
Ferdinand-Jühlke-Straße 7
99095 Erfurt, Deutschland
produktsicherheit@kolibri360.de